HAND-ME-DOWN WISDOM

Compiled by Jan Barnes

A BOOK OF TREASURED WORDS

Copper Beech Publishing

First Published in Great Britain 1990 by
Copper Beech Publishing Ltd,
East Grinstead, Sussex RH19 4HF

ISBN 0 9516295 0 6

A CIP catalogue record for this book is available from the British Library.

Acknowledgements are on page 64

Design by Ashdown Graphics
Typeset by Red Letters
Printed and bound in Great Britain by
Hillman Printers (Frome) Ltd, Frome, Somerset

Introduction

"Life's a bit like a game of bar billiards – for quite a while, you play and the balls keep coming back..then, at some point you hear a bar go down, and you have to do your best with the balls you've got left"

Alan Coren offered these words to the audience of Radio Four's Midweek programme. He was their birthday guest, celebrating his fiftieth year - and the talk had been of great influences in lives. Alan Coren recalled the bar billiard story told to him by one of his school teachers, the wisdom of which was only just becoming apparent .... 'not enough balls left to write the great novel - heard a bar come down at forty - now another at fifty'

I've always been a 'word' person - I don't analyse it - don't even think about it most of the time. I don't suppose gardeners think about plants really - they just 'know' ... but this bar billiards thing ... this hand-me-down wisdom, it sat there and it nagged away.

Why had Alan Coren remembered it all those years?

What about the man who had passed on the words all that time ago?

What words did other people carry around as their own personal Life Leaning Post?

I thought about words I've treasured most of my life and the people who had handed down the chain of thoughts and crutches ... they're quite magic, the threads of wisdom we pass around.

Communication is one of the success stories of our age.

We delight in the use of electronic mail, mobile telephones, computer networks and satellite conferencing.

Is there still room in this world of technological miracles for the real person to person call?

... the conversation which can plant the seed of determination?

... that quiet moment of discovery which can light the road for years to come?

Or are we moving too fast to recall our mother's favourite saying - the one that always used to make us smile ?

The threads of wisdom bind us all, generation to generation; they are written in autograph books, passed down in classrooms, kitchens, on long walks through the park, on chance meetings and in so many other ways.

The chains of words are everywhere providing encouragement, motivation, restraint, comfort and just good old commonsense.

This is no scientific study, but these people have offered us a unique opportunity to listen in to some of their person to person calls - that hand-me-down wisdom tucked away in a corner of the mind, waiting to be passed on ....

.... perhaps you will find yourself remembering some of these special words and linking arms with future generations by passing them on in your own way.

Jan Barnes

Alan Ayckbourn

Playwright and Theatre Director

This piece of advice was from an old Broadway producer (now dead), Michael Meyerberg.

In this (show) business
you'll either get more than you deserve
or you'll get less than you deserve
but you'll never get what you deserve

Joan Baez

Folk Singer

This motto has pulled me through many a wall of troubles and problems - it's been so appropriate for my life.

Bash on regardless!

David Bellamy

Botanist/Writer/Broadcaster

The Parable of the Talents from my father, Thomas Bellamy

- from Bob Brown, Tasmanian Wilderness Society

If you ignore your talent
you will live your life in misery,
cast out into your
own inner darkness

Think Globally Act Locally

David Blunkett

Member of Parliament, Sheffield Brightside

These words seemed very relevant when I gave up the Leadership of Sheffield City Council and entered the House of Commons as a new Backbencher - in an environment where newcomers are expected to 'know their place' - and where international, national and local political experience outside the House of Commons counts for very little with those who believe that political life begins and ends within the Palace of Westminster.

One day when you are feeling important
One day when your ego's in bloom
One day when you have the feeling
you're the most important man in the room
Take a bucket and fill it with water
Put your arm in up to the wrist
Pull it out and the hole that is left there
Is the measure of how much you'll be missed

Arthur C Clarke

Dr Clarke is very fond of the quotation from Robert Bridges' 'Testament of Beauty' which he came across about fifty years ago. Since then, he's adopted a somewhat more positive slogan, viz: 'Exploit the inevitable'.

A successful life consists of
'the masterful administration
of the unforeseen'

Exploit the inevitable

Sue Cook

Broadcaster/Writer

These words were told to me by Peter Chafer when he was editor of the programme 'Out of Court' which I used to co-present. The words were told to him by Malcolm Muggeridge.

Whenever managing a pressurised job as well as a household and family starts getting me down, or whenever I feel demoralised depressed or fainthearted, I think of those words and steel myself to carry on.

A healthy fish
always swims upstream

Ray Cooney

Writer/Actor/Director

The earliest recollection I have of being affected by words was reading my father's 'Rubaiyat of Omar Khayyam'. Although it must be among the most famous phrases in the world and therefore liable to sound trite, it is as apt today as when it was first written.

And it's very much how I've dealt with my career. No regrets. On with the next venture. But always to be aware that your actions will have an effect that you can't undo.

*'The moving finger writes
and having writ
moves on....'*

Henry Cooper OBE KSG

Former British European and Commonwealth heavyweight boxer

When I was 14 years of age, an elderly gentleman who wished to teach me boxing, a Mr Bob Hill, who today is 94 years of age, said this to me.

My twin brother and I have acted on these principles all our lives, as we feel that they not only apply to the rules of boxing, but to the rules of life.

This is a hard life
which has many bumps
and many ups and downs.
Don't go in for brawls,
behave yourself at all times and
toe the straight and narrow

Jilly Cooper

Writer

This remark by Edith Sitwell has meant a great deal to me - it means one must always try and see other peoples side of things. Jolly difficult to live up to.

This is from Mark Twain - and means that one must always be optimistic about what the future might bring. It refers to little Huckleberry Finn starting on his great trip down the Mississippi.

There is no truth,
there are only points of view

'Trust in the unexpected'

Paul Daniels

Magical Entertainer

These words were from my father '... that'll apply as much to life as to woodwork' he said.

Measure it twice son,
you'll only have to cut it once

Ronald Eyre

Theatre Director and Broadcaster

I remember, when I was in my mid-teens in the mid-40s, coming back in a bus from Leeds to Barnsley after a performance of Handel's 'Acis & Galatea' we were a small school party accompanied by my form-master who passed around the seats discussing the performance.

"So what did you think, Eyre?" he asked, reaching me.

"Well sir," I answered, "I thought it was rather trivial"

"Oh Eyre," he groaned "must you be so earnest?"

And he passed on. Bulls Eye

That night I looked in the mirror. He was quite right. Too earnest. For 45 years now I've been trying to lighten up. *Earnestly* trying to lighten up.

What's the key? I was brought up to be caring, honest, patient, conscientious - all good Methodist virtues - but nobody ever told me I was under a holy obligation to *enjoy* myself.

On the last day,
you'll be asked to account
for any good thing you* could *have
***enjoyed and* didn't**

This is a bit of jewish wisdom I shall pin on the cork board in my bathroom when I get it.

Another bullseye.

Rachael Heyhoe Flint MBE

Former England Womens Cricket Captain

I always think of the words of advice from my father and mother whenever I tackle anything in life, whether it be in my role as former international hockey and cricket player for England or county squash player and now a devotee of golf playing off 10 - and appearing in pro-ams, celeb-ams and charity golf days.

My father always told me to look the part even if I wasn't the best player; he believed that you should make every effort to turn out as smartly as possible and he would help me clean all my hockey and cricket gear the night before any match - whether it was at school level or international level.

I still relate to this now in my role as Public Relations Consultant, always look the part of a businesswoman and it makes your presence respected by your clients.

Always look the part

David Jacobs

Broadcaster

Many years ago, while holidaying in Jamaica the father of a friend of mine, seeing that I was perturbed at having a favour I had done a mutual friend come back and slap me in the face, remarked "You see, no good deed goes unpunished" - perhaps the most cynical statement I'd ever heard and, while it is not entirely true, it comes to mind time and time again.

It certainly hasn't stopped me doing good deeds as and when required, but the thought of that sentiment is often in my head and countless times it has been true.

Think about it!

You see,
no good deed goes unpunished

Derek *Jameson*

Broadcaster/Journalist

This is the philosophy which has guided my life. The words were written by the Russian revolutionary poet Mayakovsky.

"Man's dearest possession is life,
and since it is given to him to live but once,
he must so live as not to be seared
with the shame of a cowardly and trivial past,
so live that dying he can say:
'All my life and all my strengths
were given to the finest cause in the world –
the liberation of mankind' "

Bruce Kent

Peace and Human Rights Activist

These words were from my father - they have their own message.

Make friends on the way up -
you meet them all again
on the way down

Clogs to clogs in three generations

David Kossoff

Actor/Writer

The old actor recalled less momentous and profound things said to him allied in no way to bar billiards.

"Don't struggle "his father once said, "go the way you're pushed." The OA always has.

"Keep always one dream in the pocket (unfulfilled)" said his father also.

Don't struggle
go the way you're pushed

Keep always one dream in the pocket
(unfulfilled)

Don McLean

Singer/Songwriter/Composer

I have lived here in New York State for over 17 years and I have never found a more beautiful or natural area in which to dwell.

The lady who sold me the house was named Gladys Shultz and she was quite self-reliant and well read. I asked her what her secret of a long life was (she died in her 90s), and this is what she told me.

I think this is great advice!

Leave the windows wide open,
drink all the coffee you want
and avoid the neurotics

Derek Nimmo

Actor/Producer/Writer

In my youth, one way in which 'words of wisdom' seemed to be passed on from one generation to another, was through an autograph book. In those days one wrote much more than 'every good wish Cliff Richard'. One used to browse through other peoples autograph books and indeed those of ones parents and grandparents with considerable curiosity.

I know that I had written into my autograph book these two little quotations, from my grandmother, which greatly influenced me in life.

Never put off till tomorrow
that you can do today

Good better best
Never let it rest
Until the good is better
And the better best

Jonathon Porritt

Writer/Broadcaster
Former Director, Friends of the Earth

I'm not altogether certain of the origin of this phrase — some people refer to it as being a Quaker saying. I first heard it many years ago when I just started teaching, at a time when I seemed to be wandering around in quite a bit of darkness!

Since that time, I've devoted myself to lighting one or two candles here and there, and have always argued very strongly that unless each individual is prepared actively to commit himself or herself to the necessary transformation, then there is no way it is going to be achieved. Hence my suspicion of all comprehensive political ideologies!

It is better
to light one small candle
than to curse the darkness

Simon Rattle

Principal Conductor and Artistic Advisor
City of Birmingham Symphony Orchestra

When I was a teenager, John Dalby, one of the leading lights among the professors in the National Youth Orchestra, had occasion to say many wise things to me - he was, by nature, a sage. When I started my career, he sent me an unforgettable letter which ended with these words.

It has been my motto ever since!

Not only
is it better to travel than arrive,
but as a musician,
you must simply **never** *consent to arrive*

Claire Rayner

Writer and Broadcaster

I was taught these words by my grandmother as a phrase that is to be used at *all* times in your life. When things are spectacularly dreadful; when things are absolutely appalling; when everything is superb and wonderful and marvellous and happy - say these four words to yourself.

They will give you a sense of perspective and help you also to make the most of what is good and be stoical about what is bad.

This
too
will
pass

Sir Brian Rix *CBE DL*

Actor/Writer/Director
Chairman MENCAP, Vice Lord-Lieutenant of Greater London

Ovid, taught to me by my first Latin master about 55 years ago.

It seems to sum up the Protestant work ethic perfectly.

Dum vires annique sinunt tolerate labore,
jam veniet tacito curva senecta pede

(While years and strength allow,
tolerate labour, soon will come bent old age
with silent foot)

The Reverend
R*oger Royle*

Author/Broadcaster

The best advice I was ever given was by a Latin master at school when he heard that I was thinking of being ordained. It's held me in good stead, because the moment that a clergyman looks as if he has been shocked by something, then the person turns off and feels they cannot speak to him.

A clergyman
should be 'unshockable'

Donald Sinden CBE,FRSA

Actor

Caught up as I am in the hustle and bustle of urban living it was a great relief to sit back (some years ago) in a theatre to watch the Julian Slade and Dorothy Reynolds musical 'Free as Air'

The setting was one of the smaller Channel Islands where the only contact with the outside world is the boat which comes in once a week. On this day, a report comes in that the boat's arrival will be delayed for two hours. On hearing this, one of the characters (who is due to meet the boat) says "Oh good! That means we can walk slowly and take the long way round."

This has become a catch-phrase in our phrenetic household.

'Oh good!
That means we can walk slowly
and take the long way round'

Sir Cyril Smith MBE

Member of Parliament, Rochdale

There are many sayings, mottoes etc that one recalls - perhaps at the moment (being now turned 61!) especially the fact that when I told an Alderman at my first council meeting in 1972, that to reminisce was a sign of age, he replied 'Aye lad - and tha'll come to it' and ... I have!

A good thing for all to remember!

Aye lad – and tha'll come to it

The Rt Honourable
Margaret Thatcher OM FRS MP
Former Prime Minister

Mrs Thatcher's liking for these words by Sir Humphry Davy quite simply rests in the words themselves.

'Life is not made up
of great sacrifices
and duties,
but of little things;
in which smiles and kindness
given habitually
are what win and preserve
the heart and secure comfort'

Emma Thompson

Actor/Writer

My grandmother Margaret (Meggie) Moser once said this to me. It was pretty difficult to take at the time, but I've found that it's probably true and that a battered and cicatrised one serves you far better than an unshelled, unbruised one.

Your heart has to be broken
at least ten times
before it's any good
as a heart

Sue Townsend

Novelist and Playwright

Used amongst my female friends (actors, writers etc) in order to deflect the terror of a First Night.

On no account can these words be used throughout the rehearsal period or during the purdah-like pre-production time when it is essential that everyone involved *must* think that everything about the play is brilliant.

But, when everything possible has been done that can be done, ie a few hours before FIRST NIGHT, then and only then can the words be used, verbally, written on bouquets and cards and perhaps engraved on the heart.

It's only a play

Michael Winner

Film Director

I remember a particularly robust cockney film producer saying this to me when I was shortly down from Cambridge. He was referring, of course, to my not having thanked somebody in a very normal everyday situation. He was a rough diamond and I was surprised that a man should issue any instruction on manners, however right he was and however wrong I was.

I learnt from that brief moment. Not only to say 'Thank You' to people, but to think it in a more general way about all of one's life. So many people who are really quite well off and have so much to be grateful for, go through life moaning and groaning. They are not positive. Life may be imperfect for most people, but it is a great deal more imperfect for some than others.

A feeling of 'Thank You' - gratitude and appreciation - for what we do have produces a more positive and less fretful life!

It doesn't hurt to say
Thank You boy!

Acknowledgements

The author would like to thank these contributors for finding the time to share their chains of words and for their encouragement and enthusiasm. Recognition and thanks are also given to the many other people for whose contributions there is no space in this volume.

Every effort has been made to trace ownership of the quotations used in this anthology. If any omission has occurred it is inadvertent and it should be brought to the attention of the publishers.

CHAINS OF
WISDOM
MORE HAND-ME-DOWN WISDOM